My First Book of Dinosaurs

Mike Unwin

Illustrated by
Daniel Howarth

A & C BLACK
AN IMPRINT OF BLOOMSBURY
LONDON NEW DELHI NEW YORK SYDNEY

Published 2015 by A & C Black, an imprint of
Bloomsbury Publishing Plc, 50 Bedford Square
London, WC1B 3DP

www.bloomsbury.com

Bloomsbury is a registered trademark of Bloomsbury Publishing Plc

ISBN: 978-1-4729-0545-1

A CIP catalogue for this book is available from the British Library.

This book is produced using paper that is made from wood grown in managed, sustainable
forests. It is natural, renewable and recyclable. The logging and manufacturing processes
conform to the environmental regulations of the country of origin.

Printed and bound in China by Leo Paper Products

To see our full range of books
visit www.bloomsbury.com

Contents

Long before people

Dinosaurs were animals
that lived millions
of years ago, long
before people.
We know about
dinosaurs from fossils.

These are bones
that were left
in the mud when
dinosaurs died.

Scientists can work out from fossils what dinosaurs looked like and how they lived.

Around 65 million years ago, the Earth's climate suddenly changed and all dinosaurs died out.

Are you ready to meet some dinosaurs?

5

How big?

Dinosaurs came in all shapes and sizes.

 Argentinosaurus weighed as much as 15 elephants.

 Diplodocus was as long as a blue whale.

 Tyrannosaurus stood as tall as a giraffe.

 Compsognathus was only the size of a cat.

Who is it?

Do you see those lumpy rocks and boulders?

Do you dare take a closer look?

Stegosaurus
(STEG-oh-SORE-us)

It's a Stegosaurus!

This big plant eater used its spiky tail to defend itself.

It was the size of an elephant, with a brain as small as a tangerine!

8

Who is it?

Run! That dinosaur looks hungry.

Do you know what it is?

9

Allosaurus
(Al-oh-SAW-russ)

It's an Allosaurus.

This fierce hunter walked on two strong legs.

Allosaurus weighed as much as a rhino. It used its sharp, curved teeth to hunt other dinosaurs.

Who is it?

Look! Something is

What do you think it is

...ormous.
...e size of a cat.
...a very fast runner and
...ter lizards.

Who is it?

Look. Something long and wriggly
... is that a snake?

What can it be?

Diplodocus
(DIP-low-DOCK-us)

Aha! It is the long, wriggly tail of a Diplodocus.

This dinosaur measured over 30 metres from its head to the tip of its tail. That's as long as a blue whale!

Its tail helped it to balance.

Who is it?

Look at that big fin sticking out of the water.

Could it be a shark?

Ichthyosaurus
(Ick-thee-oh-SORE-us)

It isn't a shark... it's an Ichthyosaurus.

It swam underwater but came up
to breathe air, like a dolphin.

Big eyes and sharp teeth
helped it to catch fish.

Who is it?

Look! Is that a sea monster?

Plesiosaurus
(Plees-i-oh-SORE-us)

It's a Plesiosaurus.

It was not a dinosaur, but it lived at the same time.

Plesiosaurus grew as big as a crocodile. Its flippers helped it to swim fast.

Who is it?

Can you see that flash of feathers?

Were there any birds during dinosaur times?

Archaeopteryx
(ark-ee-OPT-er-ix)

Aha! It's an Archaeopteryx.

This creature was the size of a magpie.
It was one of the very first
animals to fly.

It had wings and feathers like
a bird, but a bony tail and
teeth like a dinosaur.

Who is it?

What dinosaur is this, reaching up high to nibble the top of the tree?

It must be a real giant.

Brachiosaurus
(BRAK-ee-oh-sore-us)

It's a Brachiosaurus.

This huge dinosaur had a tiny head but a very long neck. It used its height to reach the treetops, just like a giraffe does.

Who is it?

Look out! That dinosaur is swishing its tail around.

Don't stand too close or it might knock you over.

Who could it be?

Ankylosaurus
(an-KIE-loh-sore-us)

It's an Ankylosaurus.

This stocky dinosaur had a scary tail like a club.
The bone on its back gave it extra protection, like
a tortoise's shell.

Who is it?

Don't turn around! There's a huge dinosaur standing behind you.

Let's hope it doesn't step on you.

25

Argentinosaurus
(AR-gent-eeno-sore-us)

It's an Argentinosaurus.

This enormous dinosaur may have been the biggest land animal that ever lived. It was as heavy as 15 elephants!

Fossils of the Argentinosaurus were found in the South American country of Argentina.

Who is it?

What a strange head! It's big, round and knobbly.

Who do you think it is?

Pachycephalosaurus
(pack-i-KEF-al-oh-sore-russ)

It's a Pachycephalosaurus.

Stand back! They're fighting.

This dinosaur had a skull made of thick bone.
It used its head to fight.

Who is it?

This dinosaur has bent down to munch some juicy plants.

Could it be a duck?

Parasaurolophus
(pa-ra-saw-ROL-off-us)

It's a Parasaurolophus. This dinosaur had a hollow crest on its head which made its calls louder.

It ran on two legs to get away from predators.

Who is it?

This dinosaur is giving you the thumbs-up!

What can it be?

Iguanodon
(ig-WHA-noh-don)

It's an Iguanodon.

When scientists found the fossils they thought the spike was a horn on the nose.

Now they know it belonged on the thumb and helped Iguanodon to defend itself.

Who is it?

Look! Big footprints. An enormous creature has been walking across the muddy ground.

But what was it?

Tyrannosaurus
(tie-RAN-oh-sore-us)

Quick, hide! It's a Tyrannosaurus.

This huge dinosaur was the scariest creature to live on Earth.

It was heavier than an elephant, longer than a bus and had 60 sharp teeth.

Who is it?

Look out! Can you see those huge horns?

Who can it be?

Triceratops
(tri-SERRA-tops)

Triceratops means 'three-horned face'.

Its sharp horns may have helped protect it against predators. It may also have used them to show its strength — just as deer do with their antlers today.

Who is it?

Whoosh! Did you see that?

A dinosaur just ran past very fast.

What do you think it was?

Velociraptor
(vel-OSS-ee-rap-tor)

It's a Velociraptor.

This small dinosaur was the size of a dog and was very fast and fierce. Each back foot had one special long claw for hunting.

Fossils show that it had feathers, though it couldn't fly.

Who is it?

Look. Something's coming this way.

Could it be another dinosaur?

Protoceratops
(pro-toe-SERRA-tops)

It's a Protoceratops.

These small dinosaurs were the size of sheep.

They lived in herds to stay safe from predators.

Who is it?

Look! A nest full of eggs.

They're bigger than birds' eggs.

Who do you think they belong to?

Oviraptor
(OH-vee-RAP-tor)

Those eggs belong to an Oviraptor!

It used its hard beak
to eat the eggs
of other dinosaurs.
It also laid eggs
of its own.

Who is it?

Look at that in the water.

What can it be?

Spinosaurus
(SPINE-oh-SORE-us)

It's a Spinosaurus.

The colourful sail on its back made it look bigger to scare other dinosaurs.

It had long jaws full of teeth, a bit like a crocodile's.

Who is it?

Splash!

Something enormous has just grabbed a fish.

What can it be?

Pteranodon
(te-RA-no-don)

It's a Pteranodon.

This huge flying reptile had wings three times the size of a golden eagle's.

Pteranodon's long beak was perfect for scooping up fish.

Dinosaur words

climate   the usual type of weather that one place has.

fossil   remains of a dead prehistoric animal or plant, now turned to stone.

herd   a group of animals that live together.

predator   an animal that hunts other animals to eat them.

Where to see dinosaurs

You're 65 million years too late to see a living dinosaur. But today there are lots of fantastic museums where you can see enormous skeletons, life-size models, fossil footprints and even terrifying animatronic dinosaurs that roar.

For details, visit Show Me: **www.show.me.uk/dinosaurs.**

Index

 Allosaurus p10

 Compsognathus p12

 Pachycephalosaurus p28

 Spinosaurus p44

 Ankylosaurus p24

 Diplodocus p14

 Parasaurolophus p30

Stegosaurus p8

 Archaeopteryx p20

 Ichthyosaurus p16

 Plesiosaurus p18

Triceratops p36

 Argentinosaurus p26

 Iguanodon p32

 Protoceratops p40

Tyrannosaurus p34

 Brachiosaurus p22

 Oviraptor p42

 Pteranodon p46

    Velociraptor p38